AWESOME FACTS

FACTS

·FOR·

CURIOUS

KIDS

·YEAR OLDS·

Illustrated by
Andrew Pinder

Written by Steve Martin
Edited by Zoe Clark
Designed by Jade Moore
Cover design by John Bigwood

With special thanks to
Helen Cumberbatch

AWESOME FACTS

·FOR·

CURIOUS KIDS

6

·YEAR OLDS·

BUSTER BOOKS

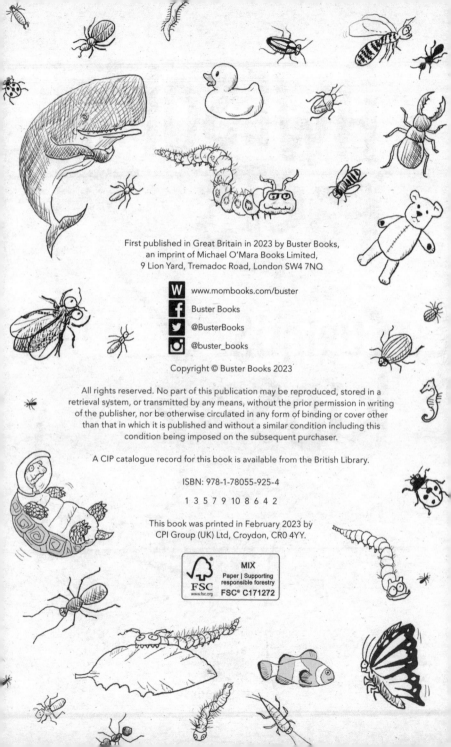

First published in Great Britain in 2023 by Buster Books,
an imprint of Michael O'Mara Books Limited,
9 Lion Yard, Tremadoc Road, London SW4 7NQ

W www.mombooks.com/buster

f Buster Books

@BusterBooks

@buster_books

A CIP catalogue record for this book is available from the British Library.

ISBN: 978-1-78055-925-4

1 3 5 7 9 10 8 6 4 2

This book was printed in February 2023 by
CPI Group (UK) Ltd, Croydon, CR0 4YY.

MIX
Paper | Supporting
responsible forestry
FSC
www.fsc.org
FSC® C171272

CONTENTS

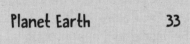

INTRODUCTION

Welcome to this totally
awesome collection of the
coolest facts for curious kids.

In this book you will learn about the country
you can walk across in 10 minutes, who won
the Great Emu War, the rubber ducks that
invaded the world and even about a cave with a
forest inside. You will also find out all about ...

★ a life-saving parrot
(page 124)

★ pink dolphins
(page 38)

★ blue sunsets
(page 51)

★ elephant babysitters
(page 71)

★ chimpanzee astronauts
(page 59)

★ ice hotels
(page 121)

Get ready to dive in and
discover all these incredible
things and more!

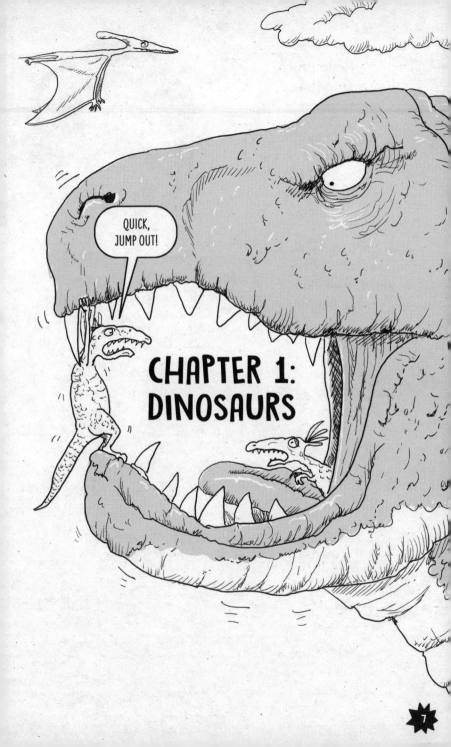

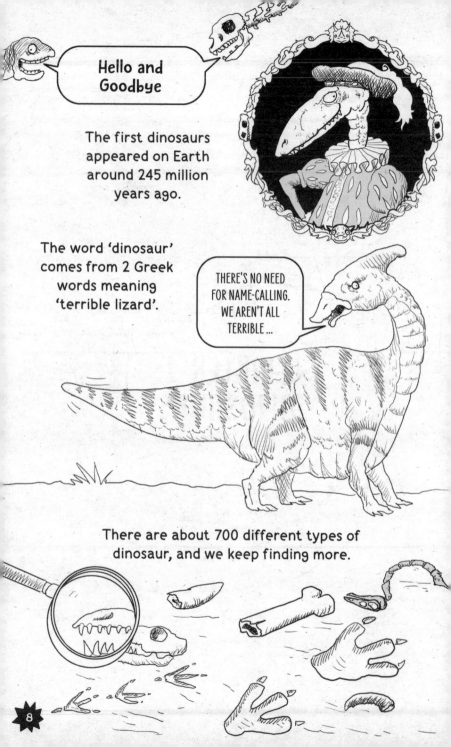

Hello and Goodbye

The first dinosaurs appeared on Earth around 245 million years ago.

The word 'dinosaur' comes from 2 Greek words meaning 'terrible lizard'.

THERE'S NO NEED FOR NAME-CALLING. WE AREN'T ALL TERRIBLE...

There are about 700 different types of dinosaur, and we keep finding more.

Dinosaurs lived on every continent on Earth, including Antarctica.

Dinosaurs became extinct about 66 million years ago. Early humans appeared only around 6 million years ago, so dinosaurs and people never met.

Nobody knows for certain why all the dinosaurs disappeared. Some scientists think it was because a huge asteroid (a space rock) crashed into Earth.

Teeth, Claws, Horns and Spikes

I USE MY LONG CLAWS TO REACH THE LEAVES IN THE TREES. I'M A VEGETARIAN!

The claws of a *Therizinosaurus* were 1 metre (3.2 feet) long. That's as long as a sword.

The plant-eating *Nigersaurus* had more than 500 teeth.

T. rex had about 60 teeth, which could be up to 30 centimetres (12 inches) long. This fierce animal had no problem ripping up its food.

The name *Triceratops* means '3-horned face'. This dinosaur's horns could grow to up to 90 centimetres (3 feet) in length.

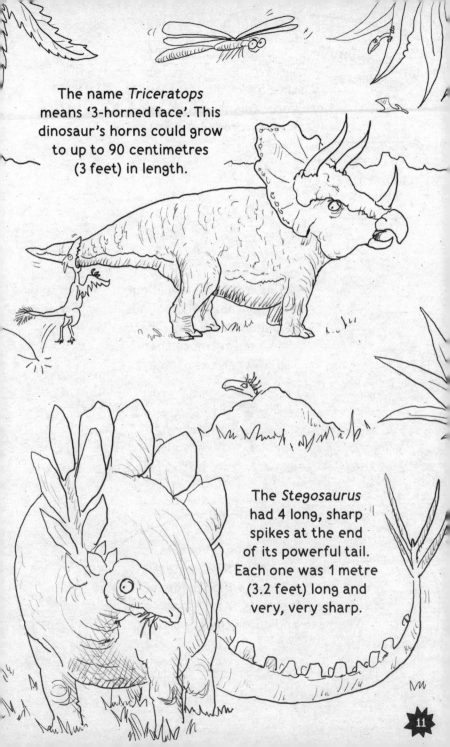

The *Stegosaurus* had 4 long, sharp spikes at the end of its powerful tail. Each one was 1 metre (3.2 feet) long and very, very sharp.

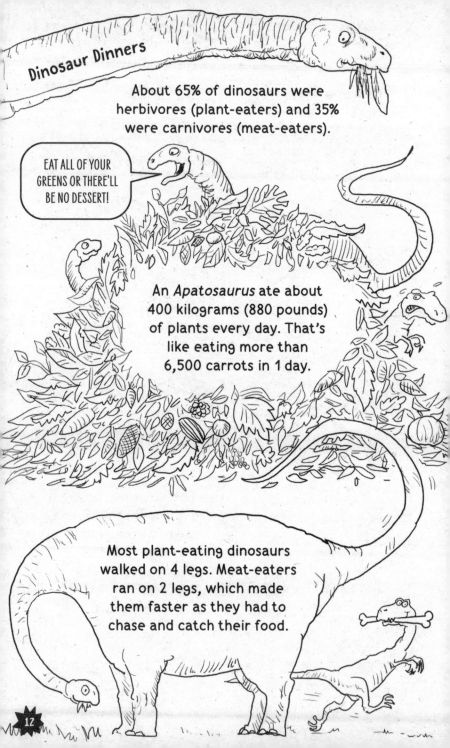

Dinosaur Dinners

About 65% of dinosaurs were herbivores (plant-eaters) and 35% were carnivores (meat-eaters).

EAT ALL OF YOUR GREENS OR THERE'LL BE NO DESSERT!

An *Apatosaurus* ate about 400 kilograms (880 pounds) of plants every day. That's like eating more than 6,500 carrots in 1 day.

Most plant-eating dinosaurs walked on 4 legs. Meat-eaters ran on 2 legs, which made them faster as they had to chase and catch their food.

DINNER TIME!

A meat-guzzling *T. rex* was so mean and scary, it would even enjoy feasting on ... another *T. rex*.

About 93 million years ago, giant crocodiles loved nothing more than a meal of fresh dinosaur.

GULP!

Britain's National Poo Museum has some 120-million-year-old dinosaur poo on display.

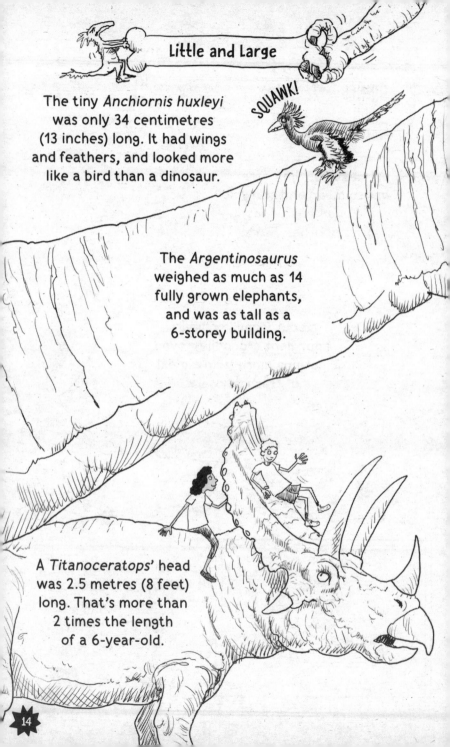

Little and Large

The tiny *Anchiornis huxleyi* was only 34 centimetres (13 inches) long. It had wings and feathers, and looked more like a bird than a dinosaur.

SQUAWK!

The *Argentinosaurus* weighed as much as 14 fully grown elephants, and was as tall as a 6-storey building.

A *Titanoceratops'* head was 2.5 metres (8 feet) long. That's more than 2 times the length of a 6-year-old.

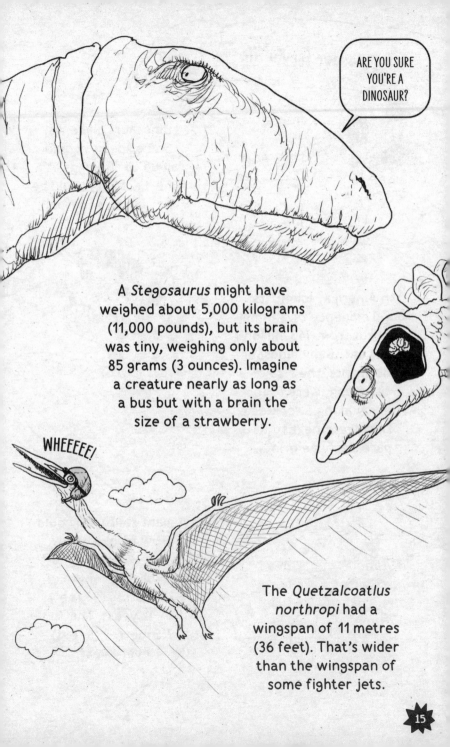

ARE YOU SURE YOU'RE A DINOSAUR?

A *Stegosaurus* might have weighed about 5,000 kilograms (11,000 pounds), but its brain was tiny, weighing only about 85 grams (3 ounces). Imagine a creature nearly as long as a bus but with a brain the size of a strawberry.

WHEEEE!

The *Quetzalcoatlus northropi* had a wingspan of 11 metres (36 feet). That's wider than the wingspan of some fighter jets.

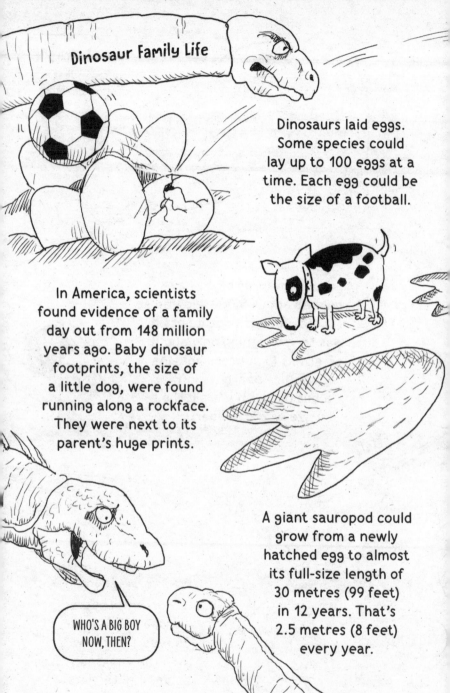

Dinosaur Family Life

Dinosaurs laid eggs. Some species could lay up to 100 eggs at a time. Each egg could be the size of a football.

In America, scientists found evidence of a family day out from 148 million years ago. Baby dinosaur footprints, the size of a little dog, were found running along a rockface. They were next to its parent's huge prints.

WHO'S A BIG BOY NOW, THEN?

A giant sauropod could grow from a newly hatched egg to almost its full-size length of 30 metres (99 feet) in 12 years. That's 2.5 metres (8 feet) every year.

'Big Mama' is the name that scientists gave to a 75-million-year-old dinosaur fossil found sitting on top of a nest of eggs in a desert in Mongolia.

I HOPE I LOOK AS SCARY AS YOU WHEN I GROW UP, MUM.

Some dinosaurs lived in big groups called herds. Scientists in Argentina found fossils from 80 different *Mussaurus* dinosaurs in the same place.

FANCY SEEING YOU HERE!

HOW ARE THE KIDS?

I LOVE MY HERD!

The Fast and the Slow

Ornithomimids could run at 80 kilometres (50 miles) per hour. That's faster than a car driving on a main road.

ZOOOOOM!

All dinosaurs had tails. If they didn't, they would have toppled over when they ran. The tails helped them to keep their balance.

WHERE'S MY TAIL GONE?!

The huge *Argentinosaurus* weighed 70,000 kilograms (154,000 pounds) and could only move at 8 kilometres (5 miles) per hour. That's about the same speed as a fast-walking human.

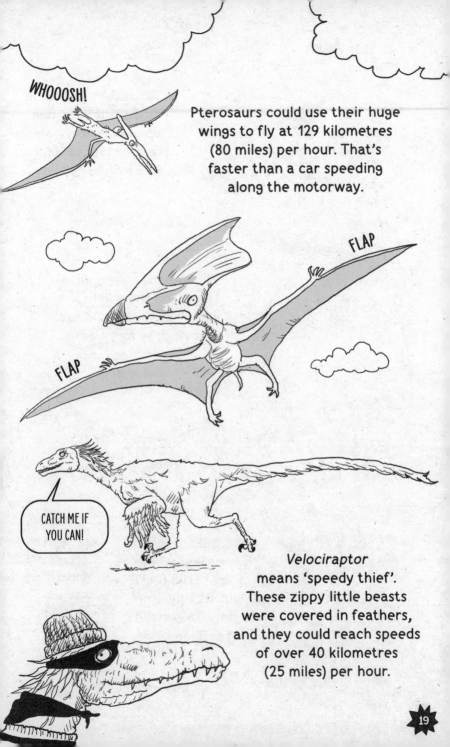

WHOOOSH!

Pterosaurs could use their huge wings to fly at 129 kilometres (80 miles) per hour. That's faster than a car speeding along the motorway.

FLAP

FLAP

CATCH ME IF YOU CAN!

Velociraptor means 'speedy thief'. These zippy little beasts were covered in feathers, and they could reach speeds of over 40 kilometres (25 miles) per hour.

T. Rex

A *T. rex* that scientists named 'Sue' was dug up in America. Her skeleton was sold for 8.36 million dollars.

T. rex bones were hollow. This made them lighter and faster so they could catch their prey more easily.

A *T. rex*'s legs were 3.5 metres (11.5 feet) long, but its tiny arms were only 0.9 metres (3 feet) long.

PHEW, I DON'T THINK HE'S SEEN US YET ...

CHAPTER 2:
SCIENCE

Mighty Materials

MORE OF THESE STRANGE FOSSILS, SIR.

ARCH AEO MKII

It takes 200 years for a plastic straw to rot away.

Metal objects get bigger when they get hot. That's why the Eiffel Tower in France grows 15 centimetres (6 inches) taller in summer.

I'VE BEEN CLIMBING FOR DAYS AND I STILL CAN'T REACH THE TOP!

TIME TO GROW AGAIN!

A type of plant called bamboo can grow up to 91 centimetres (36 inches) every day.

Wool clothes will keep you warm in winter and cool in summer. Wool is even thought to be fireproof.

IT'S A GOOD JOB OUR FLEECE WILL HAVE GROWN BACK IN 6 WEEKS ...

A diamond is so hard, the only thing that can cut it is another diamond.

FREEDOM!

WHEE!

WHEE!

It's so hot deep underground that rocks melt. This hot liquid sometimes bursts out of the top of a volcano and flows down the sides. This is called lava.

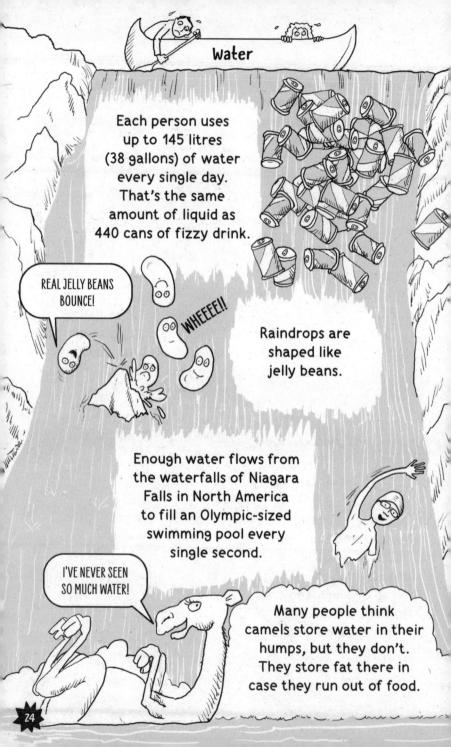

Water

Each person uses up to 145 litres (38 gallons) of water every single day. That's the same amount of liquid as 440 cans of fizzy drink.

REAL JELLY BEANS BOUNCE!

WHEEEE!!

Raindrops are shaped like jelly beans.

Enough water flows from the waterfalls of Niagara Falls in North America to fill an Olympic-sized swimming pool every single second.

I'VE NEVER SEEN SO MUCH WATER!

Many people think camels store water in their humps, but they don't. They store fat there in case they run out of food.

When it's cold, water falls to Earth as snow. Although snow looks white, it's actually see-through.

Every snowflake has 6 sides, but every snowflake looks different.

CHILLIN' ...

Water gets bigger when it freezes and turns into ice.

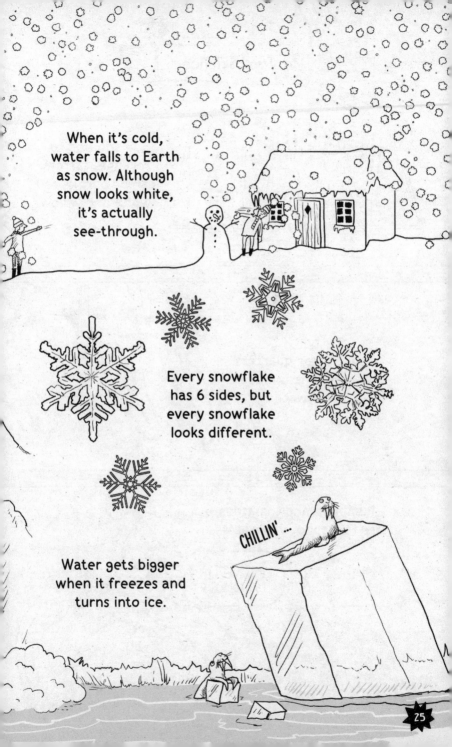

Food Science

In addition to orange, carrots can be purple, red, white and yellow.

About three quarters of a banana is made up of water.

Pumpkins and tomatoes are fruits, not vegetables.

IT'S BECAUSE WE CONTAIN SEEDS!

Corn is used in hundreds of different ways. Besides making tasty breakfast cereals, it's used to produce glue, carpets and crayons.

SQUEAK

WHEEE!

SQUEAK

There are over 7,500 different types of apple in the world, and over 3,000 different types of pear.

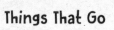

Things That Go

A large passenger plane needs about 12 litres of fuel to fly 1 kilometre (5 gallons per mile). A car travels about 200 times further using the same amount of fuel.

ZOOOOOOOM!

WHIRRRR! WHIRRRR!

A helicopter's blades spin in a circle up to 500 times every minute.

The *Titanic* was a famous passenger ship that sank in 1912. It had 4 funnels, but only 3 of them worked. The fourth was just to make the ship look cooler.

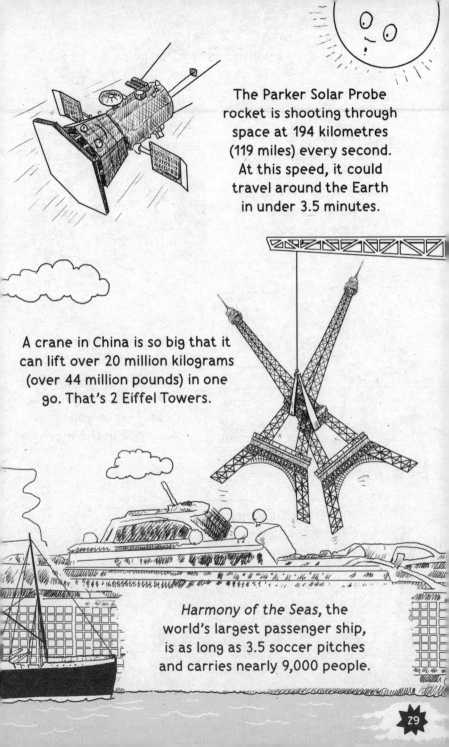

The Parker Solar Probe rocket is shooting through space at 194 kilometres (119 miles) every second. At this speed, it could travel around the Earth in under 3.5 minutes.

A crane in China is so big that it can lift over 20 million kilograms (over 44 million pounds) in one go. That's 2 Eiffel Towers.

Harmony of the Seas, the world's largest passenger ship, is as long as 3.5 soccer pitches and carries nearly 9,000 people.

Inventions

The first electronic computer was invented in 1946. It was bigger than a school classroom and weighed about the same as 2 buses.

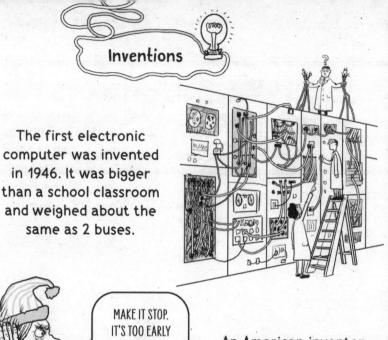

An American inventor made an alarm clock over 200 years ago. The problem was it could only wake you up at 4 o'clock in the morning.

Traffic lights were introduced in 1868 ... 18 years before the car was invented.

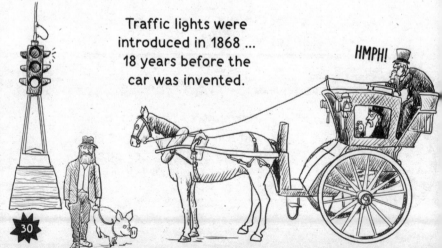

Tomato ketchup was once used as a medicine. Its creator, Dr Bennett, claimed it could cure everything from an upset tummy to aching bones. It didn't.

The first bicycles didn't have any pedals. Cyclists had to push themselves along the road with their feet.

The Science of TV

A picture on a TV screen is made up of dots so tiny that you can't see them. They're called pixels and there can be millions of them on 1 screen.

A TV screen shows about 24 different 'photographs' every second. They change so fast, the pictures look like moving images.

TV signals carry the video and sound information that is displayed as a moving picture on your TV screen. TV signals move so quickly, they can travel around the Earth 7 times in less than 1 second.

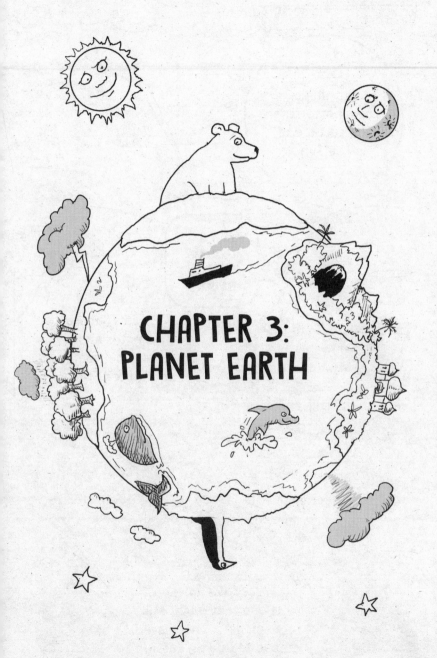

CHAPTER 3:
PLANET EARTH

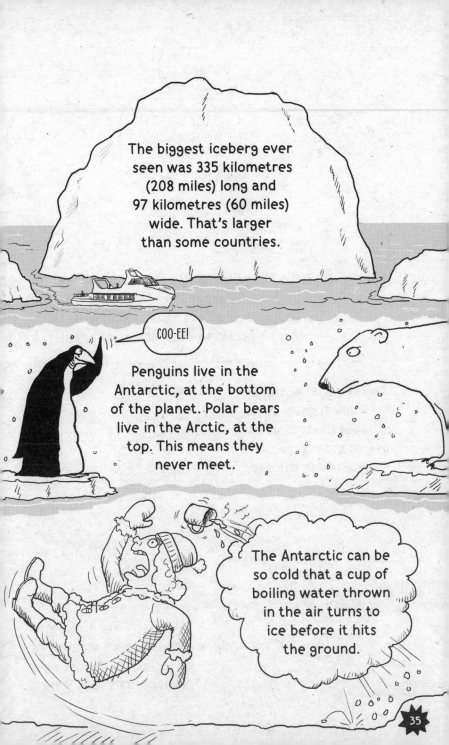

The biggest iceberg ever seen was 335 kilometres (208 miles) long and 97 kilometres (60 miles) wide. That's larger than some countries.

COO-EE!

Penguins live in the Antarctic, at the bottom of the planet. Polar bears live in the Arctic, at the top. This means they never meet.

The Antarctic can be so cold that a cup of boiling water thrown in the air turns to ice before it hits the ground.

35

Oceans

THESE DUCKS AREN'T VERY FRIENDLY. THEY NEVER SAY HELLO ...

During a storm in 1992, a ship lost its cargo of about 29,000 rubber ducks. They've turned up on beaches all over the world, from the frozen Arctic to Australia and Japan.

The sea is 11 kilometres (7 miles) deep at its deepest part. That's the height that large planes fly up to in the sky.

HI THERE!

Between Greenland and Iceland, there's an undersea waterfall that's just over 3.5 kilometres (2 miles) tall.

The Pacific Ocean is huge. At its widest part, it would take about 8 months to cross it in a pedalo.

About 97% of the Earth's water can be found in its oceans. Water covers about 71% of the surface of our planet.

The largest animal in the ocean – or anywhere else – is the blue whale. It's as long as 3 school buses and weighs as much as 20 of them!

Rainforests

Rainforests are brilliant for explorers. They are home to about 50% of the world's plant and animal species.

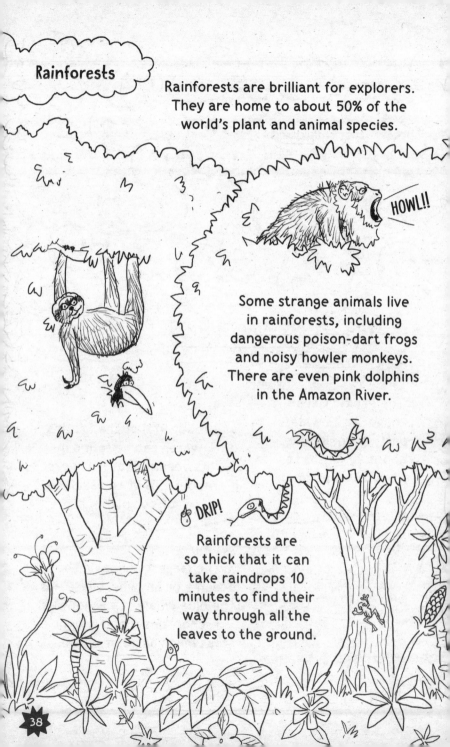

HOWL!!

Some strange animals live in rainforests, including dangerous poison-dart frogs and noisy howler monkeys. There are even pink dolphins in the Amazon River.

DRIP!

Rainforests are so thick that it can take raindrops 10 minutes to find their way through all the leaves to the ground.

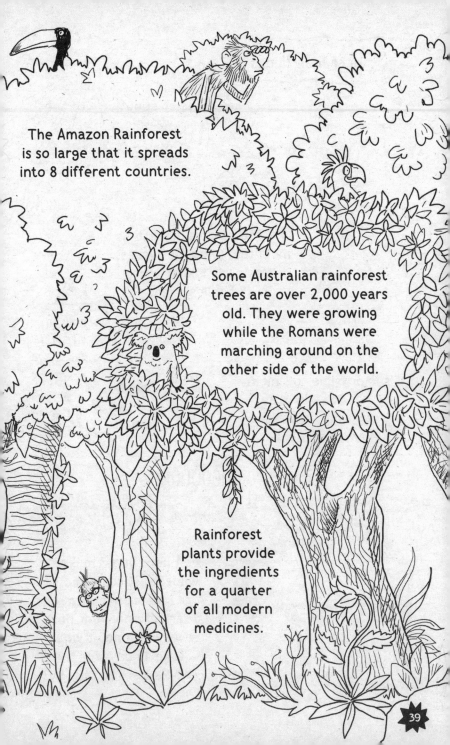

The Amazon Rainforest is so large that it spreads into 8 different countries.

Some Australian rainforest trees are over 2,000 years old. They were growing while the Romans were marching around on the other side of the world.

Rainforest plants provide the ingredients for a quarter of all modern medicines.

39

Incredible Places

The world's highest mountain is Mount Everest. It's nearly 9 kilometres (5.5 miles) high.

PASS THE SALT, PLEASE?

It's impossible to sink in the Dead Sea in Israel. It's so salty, it makes everything float.

ZOOOOOOM!

A herd of 1.5 million wildebeest roams across Africa's Serengeti National Park. If one went past every second, it would take 18 days for the whole herd to pass by.

The Nile is the longest river in the world. It would take almost 3 months to swim non-stop from one end to the other.

YOU CAN DO IT!

There is no land at the North Pole (the Earth's most northern point). It lies on floating ice.

Devon Island in Canada is as large as some countries, but no one lives there. In fact, the conditions are so harsh that astronauts go there to practise being on Mars.

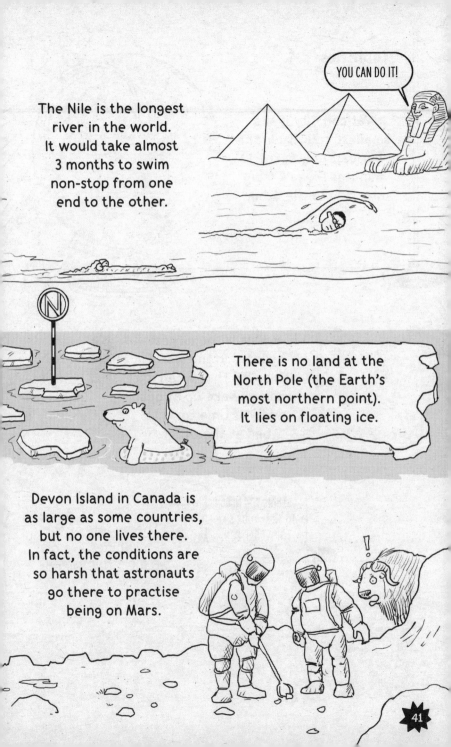

Countries

Vatican City is the smallest country in the world. It only takes 10 minutes to walk from one side to the other.

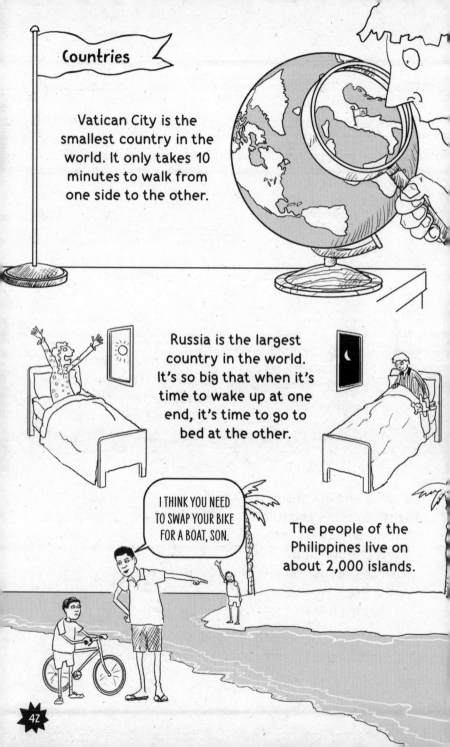

Russia is the largest country in the world. It's so big that when it's time to wake up at one end, it's time to go to bed at the other.

I THINK YOU NEED TO SWAP YOUR BIKE FOR A BOAT, SON.

The people of the Philippines live on about 2,000 islands.

The country of Iceland has no trains at all.

Over a quarter of land in the Netherlands is lower than the sea. Huge walls (called dykes) have been built to keep the sea out.

More than 40 countries still have kings and queens, including Britain, Spain, Thailand and Morocco.

GA-GA

43

Wild Weather

Thunder travels 1 kilometre in 3 seconds (1 mile in 5 seconds). After lightning, count until you hear the thunder to work out how far away the storm is.

YIKES!

I COULD DO WITH A DRINK!

Some parts of the Atacama Desert in South America once went without rain for 400 years.

Places in the far north have very long days and nights. In parts of Alaska, the Sun doesn't set for over 2 months in the summer, and it's night-time for 2 months in winter.

WHY HAVE YOU WOKEN ME UP IN THE MIDDLE OF THE NIGHT? I'VE ONLY HAD A FEW WEEKS' SLEEP.

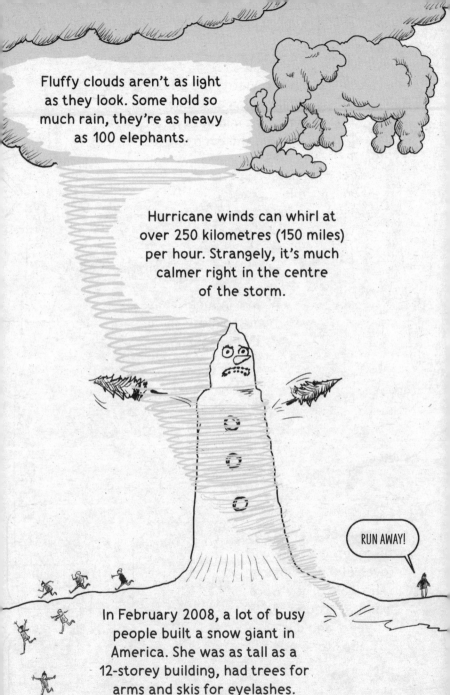

Fluffy clouds aren't as light as they look. Some hold so much rain, they're as heavy as 100 elephants.

Hurricane winds can whirl at over 250 kilometres (150 miles) per hour. Strangely, it's much calmer right in the centre of the storm.

RUN AWAY!

In February 2008, a lot of busy people built a snow giant in America. She was as tall as a 12-storey building, had trees for arms and skis for eyelashes.

Caves

A cave in Vietnam is 9 kilometres (5.5 miles) long and taller than the largest pyramid in Egypt. It has a lake, a river and even a forest inside.

FLAP!

FLAP!

FLAP!

A cave in America is home to more than 15 million bats.

A group of French boys discovered a cave with over 600 paintings on the walls. They were painted around 17,000 years ago during the Stone Age.

The Moon

OUCH! MY FEET ARE SO SORE...

The Moon is about 385,000 kilometres (239,000 miles) away. If you were to set off on your 7th birthday and walked non-stop, you'd be 16 years old when you arrived.

BOING!

You weigh 6 times less on the Moon.

The Sun is about 400 times bigger than the Moon. It's also about 400 times further away. That's why the Sun and the Moon look the same size from Earth.

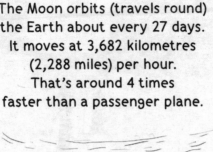

The Moon orbits (travels round) the Earth about every 27 days. It moves at 3,682 kilometres (2,288 miles) per hour. That's around 4 times faster than a passenger plane.

The Moon and Earth are always pulling towards each other. The pull of the Moon affects the rising and falling of the planet's oceans.

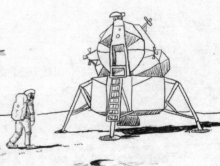

Neil Armstrong was the first man to step on to the Moon in 1969. Because there isn't any wind on the Moon, his footprints are still there in the dust.

Mars

Mars has icy north and south poles, just like Earth.

WHAT ARE YOU GUYS DOING HERE?

Mars is rusty. The rusty iron dust on its surface makes the planet look reddish-brown.

HERE, TAKE ONE OF US!

There are robot cars driving around Mars taking photos. They are steered from Earth, 225 million kilometres (140 million miles) away.

On Mars, sunsets are blue.

Earth is about 2 times the size of Mars but is 10 times heavier.

Olympus Mons is a volcano on Mars. It is almost 3 times higher than the biggest mountain on Earth.

The Planets

MERCURY

EARTH

SUN

VENUS

There are 8 planets
travelling around the
Sun in our solar system:
Mercury, Venus, Earth,
Mars, Jupiter, Saturn,
Uranus and Neptune.

MARS

Saturn has over
80 moons, but
Mercury and Venus
don't have any.

There are 7
rings around Saturn.
They are made of
ice and rock.

SATURN

Uranus stinks. The whole planet smells of rotten eggs.

JUPITER

URANUS

IT WASN'T ME!

Jupiter is the largest planet in our solar system. More than 1,300 Earths could fit inside it.

NEPTUNE

Neptune is so far away that a spacecraft sent from Earth across the solar system took 12 years to travel near to it.

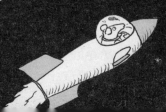

Space Weather

There is a hurricane on Jupiter that has been blowing for over 200 years. The storm is 2 times the size of Earth and has winds of 644 kilometres (400 miles) per hour.

DON'T WORRY, IT'LL PASS IN A FEW MONTHS!

Mars is covered in dust. Sometimes huge dust storms blow over the entire planet and last for months.

Wind from the Sun is called solar wind. It can travel at over 1.6 million kilometres (1 million miles) per hour.

Scientists look at the weather in space to help them forecast what the weather will be like on Earth.

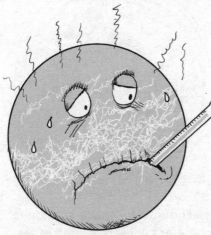

Venus is nearly 5 times hotter than boiling water.

One of Jupiter's moons is covered in ice up to 24 kilometres (15 miles) thick. Scientists think that there's an ocean under all the ice.

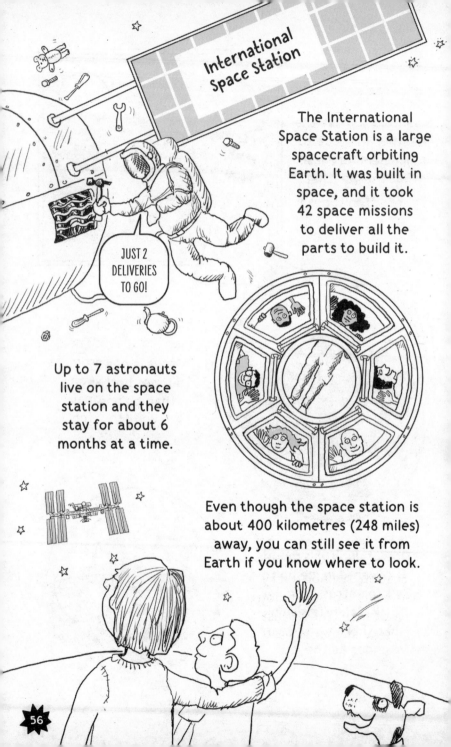

International Space Station

The International Space Station is a large spacecraft orbiting Earth. It was built in space, and it took 42 space missions to deliver all the parts to build it.

JUST 2 DELIVERIES TO GO!

Up to 7 astronauts live on the space station and they stay for about 6 months at a time.

Even though the space station is about 400 kilometres (248 miles) away, you can still see it from Earth if you know where to look.

The International Space Station travels at almost 29,000 kilometres (18,000 miles) per hour and goes around the Earth 16 times a day.

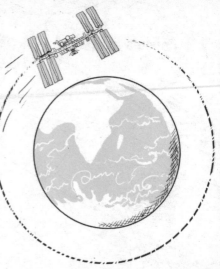

Buzz Lightyear has been to space. The action figure from *Toy Story* lived on the International Space Station for 15 months.

If you get homesick on the International Space Station, try not to cry. The tears won't run down your face. They'll just stay in your eyes.

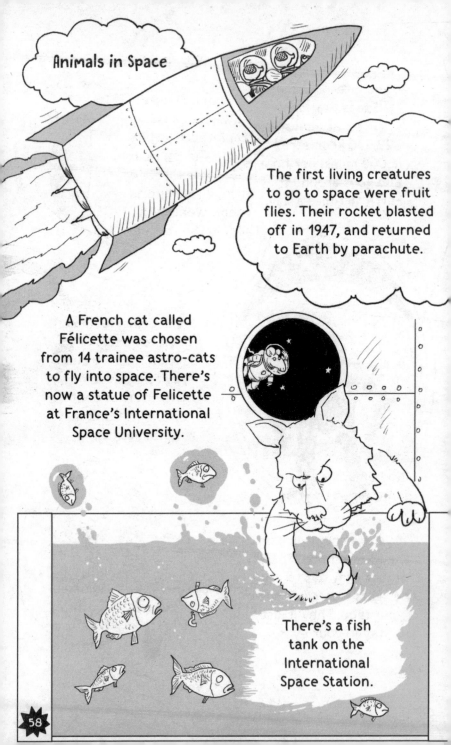

Animals in Space

The first living creatures to go to space were fruit flies. Their rocket blasted off in 1947, and returned to Earth by parachute.

A French cat called Félicette was chosen from 14 trainee astro-cats to fly into space. There's now a statue of Felicette at France's International Space University.

There's a fish tank on the International Space Station.

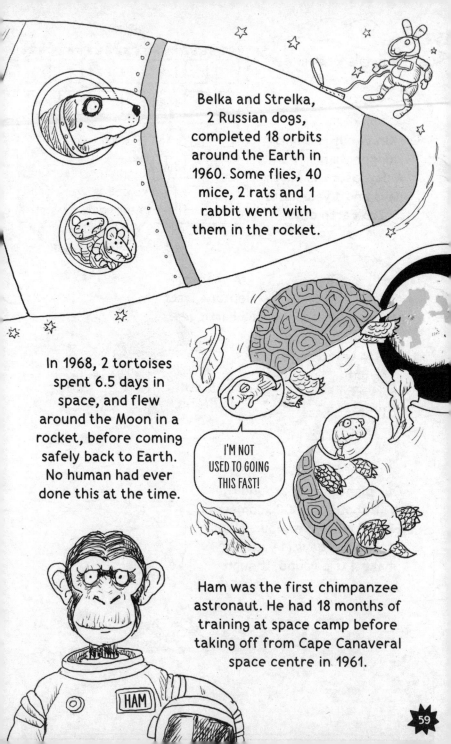

Belka and Strelka, 2 Russian dogs, completed 18 orbits around the Earth in 1960. Some flies, 40 mice, 2 rats and 1 rabbit went with them in the rocket.

In 1968, 2 tortoises spent 6.5 days in space, and flew around the Moon in a rocket, before coming safely back to Earth. No human had ever done this at the time.

I'M NOT USED TO GOING THIS FAST!

Ham was the first chimpanzee astronaut. He had 18 months of training at space camp before taking off from Cape Canaveral space centre in 1961.

HAM

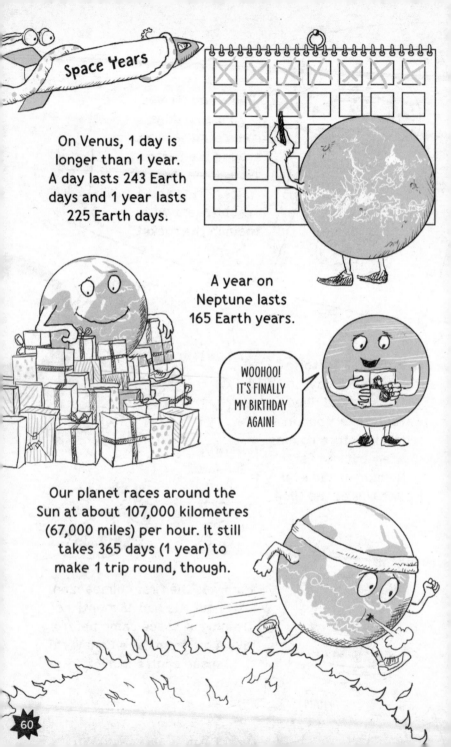

Space Years

On Venus, 1 day is longer than 1 year. A day lasts 243 Earth days and 1 year lasts 225 Earth days.

A year on Neptune lasts 165 Earth years.

WOOHOO! IT'S FINALLY MY BIRTHDAY AGAIN!

Our planet races around the Sun at about 107,000 kilometres (67,000 miles) per hour. It still takes 365 days (1 year) to make 1 trip round, though.

CHAPTER 5: ANIMALS

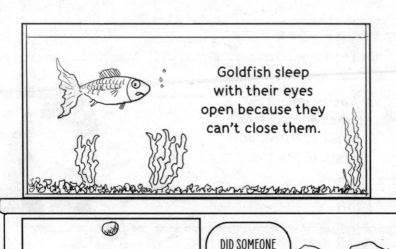

Goldfish sleep with their eyes open because they can't close them.

Dogs are brilliant at smelling. They can pick up pongs from over 1.5 kilometres (1 mile) away. That's a 20-minute walk!

DID SOMEONE SAY "WALK"?!

A rabbit's teeth never stop growing. If they didn't wear them down with lots of chewing, they'd grow up to 13 centimetres (5 inches) every year.

On the Farm

NOW, WHERE DID I LEAVE THE SOAP?

Each year, a cow makes enough milk to fill 45 bathtubs right to the top.

Sheep have 4 stomachs. So do cows and goats.

There are about 4 times more chickens in the world than people.

I CAN'T PUT THIS BOOK DOWN!

Pigs are very clever. They're smarter than a 3-year-old child.

A horse can swivel its ears around to help it to hear better.

Our eyes have round pupils (the black opening in the centre of the eye), but a goat's pupils are rectangular.

Lions

A lion's roar is so loud you can hear it from 8 kilometres (5 miles) away. That's at least a 90-minute walk away.

There are 24 hours in a day and lions can sleep for up to 20 of them.

Male lions have manes (thick hair around their necks). Females don't.

YUMMY!

Lions love eating meat. They eat the same amount as about 60 burgers every day.

Lions can see really well in the dark. That's why they like to hunt at night.

Lions can open their mouths so wide they could fit 2 adult-sized heads inside.

Tigers

AW, WHAT A CUTE LITTLE KITTY!

Tigers are the largest cats in the world. They're even bigger than lions.

You won't see 2 tigers with the same markings. Each tiger's stripes are different.

There are no tigers in Africa. Most live in India.

WHEE!!!

A tiger can run as fast as a racehorse and jump the length of 2 cars parked next to each other.

Most cats hate water, but tigers love swimming.

GO AWAY!

Lions enjoy living together, but tigers like to be on their own.

Elephants

An elephant's tusks never stop growing. The larger the tusks, the older the elephant.

Elephants say "Hello" to each other by wrapping their trunks together.

HI, THERE!

An elephant can walk along the bottom of a river and use its trunk as a snorkel.

Elephant mums sometimes leave their young with elephant babysitters.

Elephants cover themselves in cooling, wet mud to protect themselves from the Sun's hot rays.

An elephant produces over 100 kilograms (220 pounds) of poo every day. That's more than the weight of a sofa.

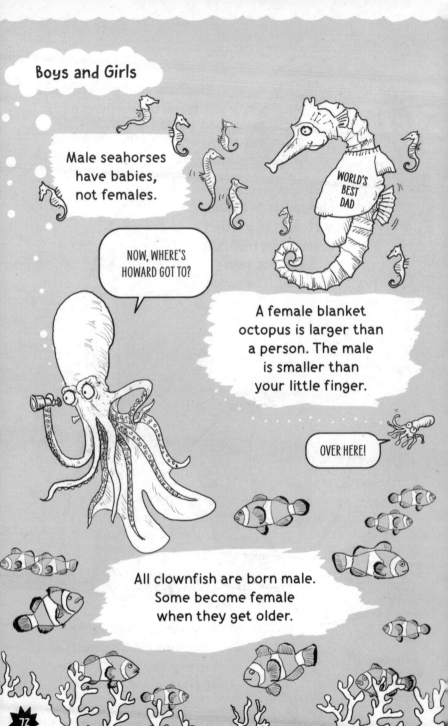

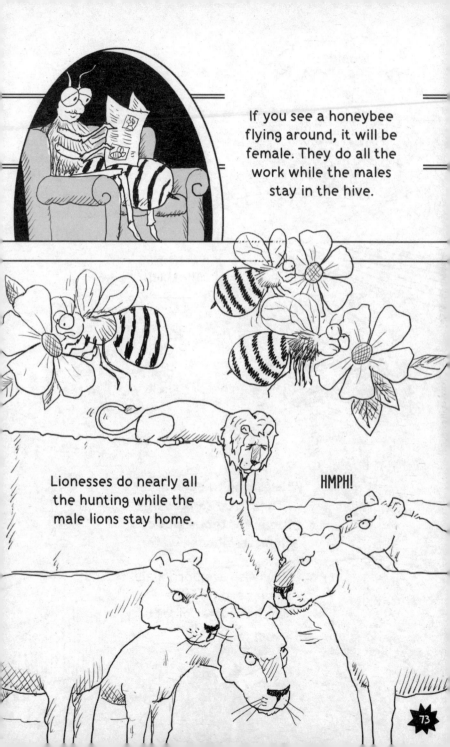

If you see a honeybee flying around, it will be female. They do all the work while the males stay in the hive.

Lionesses do nearly all the hunting while the male lions stay home.

HMPH!

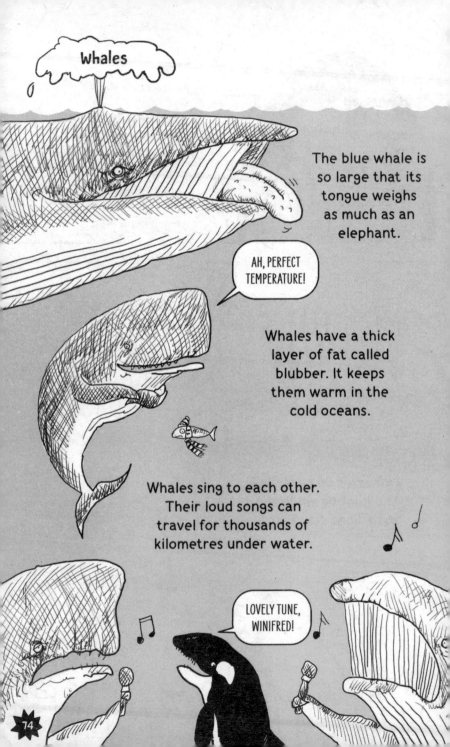

Whales

The blue whale is so large that its tongue weighs as much as an elephant.

AH, PERFECT TEMPERATURE!

Whales have a thick layer of fat called blubber. It keeps them warm in the cold oceans.

Whales sing to each other. Their loud songs can travel for thousands of kilometres under water.

LOVELY TUNE, WINIFRED!

CHAPTER 6:
MINIBEASTS

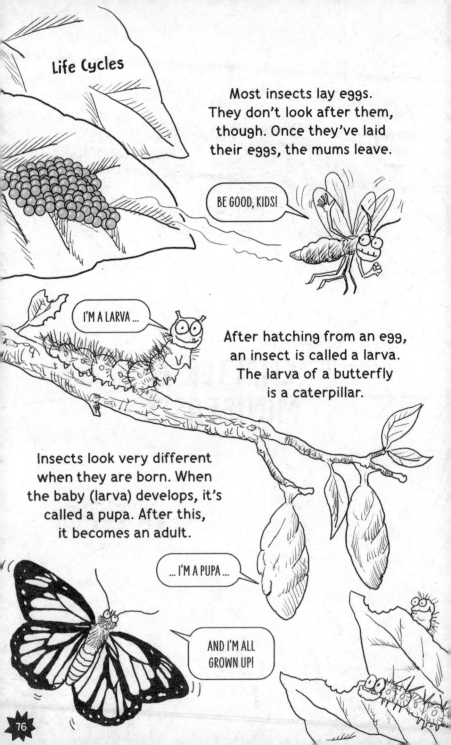

Life Cycles

Most insects lay eggs. They don't look after them, though. Once they've laid their eggs, the mums leave.

BE GOOD, KIDS!

I'M A LARVA ...

After hatching from an egg, an insect is called a larva. The larva of a butterfly is a caterpillar.

Insects look very different when they are born. When the baby (larva) develops, it's called a pupa. After this, it becomes an adult.

... I'M A PUPA ...

AND I'M ALL GROWN UP!

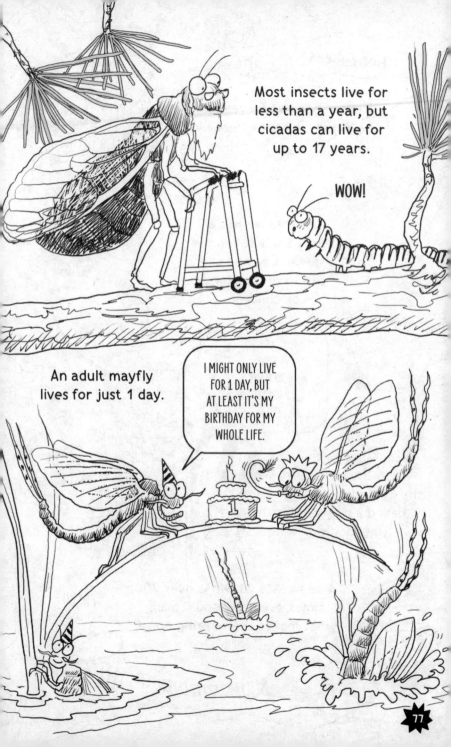

Honeybees

A honeybee has 5 eyes and the 2 largest ones are hairy.

Every hive has a mum. She's called the queen bee and she can have thousands of children.

IT'S JUST AS WELL I HAVE 5 EYES WITH SO MANY KIDS TO KEEP AN EYE ON.

A bee beats its wings over 200 times every second. This is what makes the buzzing noise.

PHEW!

BUUZZZZZZZZZZZZZZZ

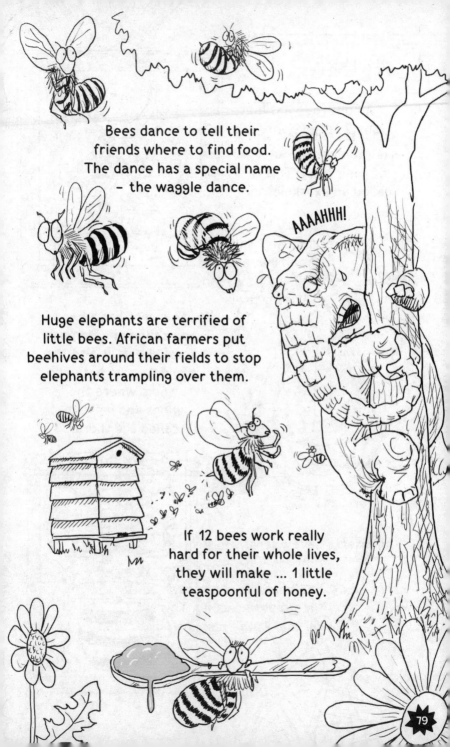

Bees dance to tell their friends where to find food. The dance has a special name – the waggle dance.

AAAAHHH!

Huge elephants are terrified of little bees. African farmers put beehives around their fields to stop elephants trampling over them.

If 12 bees work really hard for their whole lives, they will make ... 1 little teaspoonful of honey.

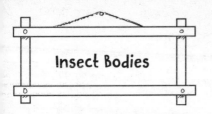

Insect Bodies

All insects have their skeleton on the outside of their body. This is called an exoskeleton.

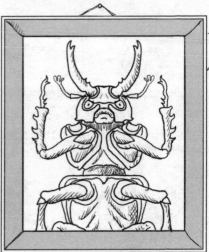

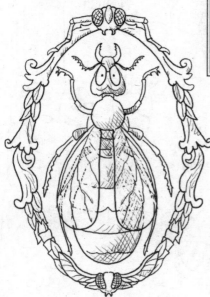

An insect has a head and abdomen (stomach area) like us. It also has a middle part between them where the wings and legs are, called the thorax.

All insects have 6 legs.

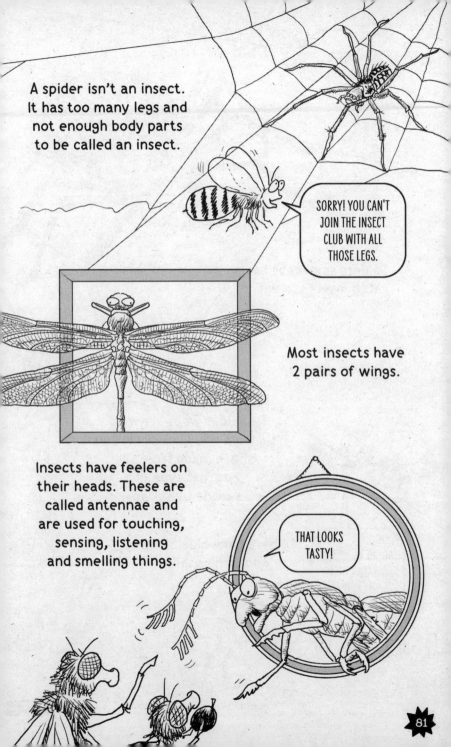

A spider isn't an insect. It has too many legs and not enough body parts to be called an insect.

SORRY! YOU CAN'T JOIN THE INSECT CLUB WITH ALL THOSE LEGS.

Most insects have 2 pairs of wings.

Insects have feelers on their heads. These are called antennae and are used for touching, sensing, listening and smelling things.

THAT LOOKS TASTY!

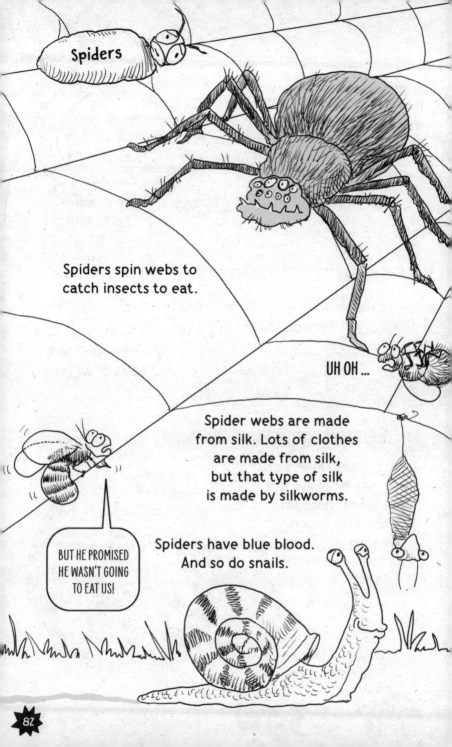

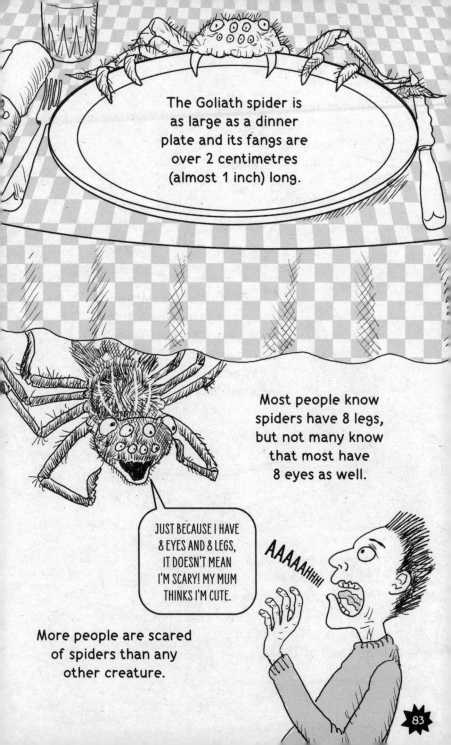

The Goliath spider is as large as a dinner plate and its fangs are over 2 centimetres (almost 1 inch) long.

Most people know spiders have 8 legs, but not many know that most have 8 eyes as well.

JUST BECAUSE I HAVE 8 EYES AND 8 LEGS, IT DOESN'T MEAN I'M SCARY! MY MUM THINKS I'M CUTE.

AAAAAHHH!

More people are scared of spiders than any other creature.

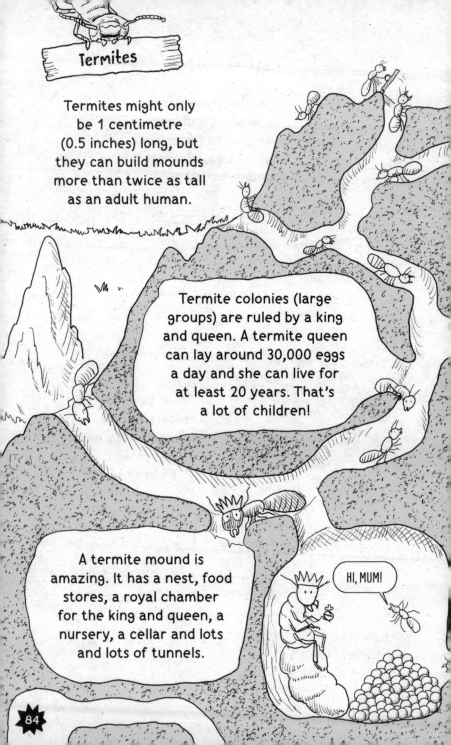

Termites

Termites might only be 1 centimetre (0.5 inches) long, but they can build mounds more than twice as tall as an adult human.

Termite colonies (large groups) are ruled by a king and queen. A termite queen can lay around 30,000 eggs a day and she can live for at least 20 years. That's a lot of children!

A termite mound is amazing. It has a nest, food stores, a royal chamber for the king and queen, a nursery, a cellar and lots and lots of tunnels.

HI, MUM!

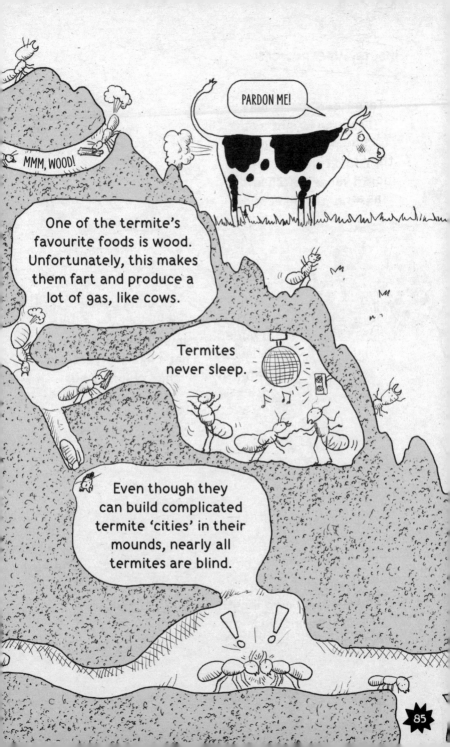

Insect Superpowers

If a tiger beetle was the same height as a 6-year-old child, it could run the length of a soccer pitch and back in just 1 second.

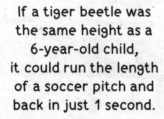

A dung beetle can move over 1,000 times its own weight. That's like a 6-year-old child pulling a bus full of people.

A flea can jump up to 200 times its own length. That's like a 6-year-old child leaping the length of 2 soccer pitches.

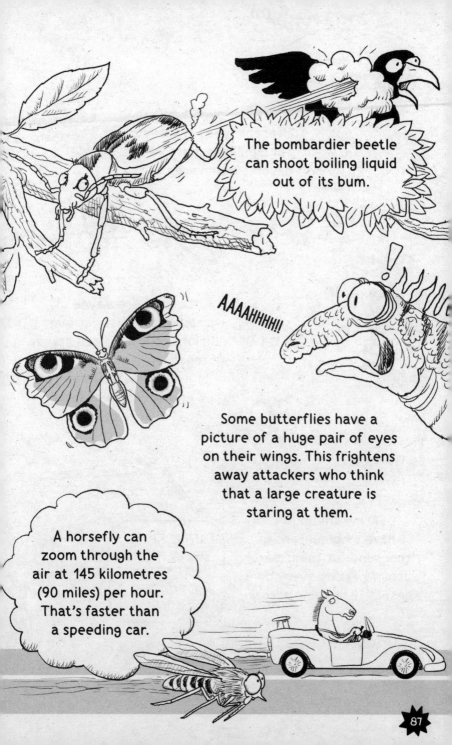

The bombardier beetle can shoot boiling liquid out of its bum.

AAAAHHHH!!

Some butterflies have a picture of a huge pair of eyes on their wings. This frightens away attackers who think that a large creature is staring at them.

A horsefly can zoom through the air at 145 kilometres (90 miles) per hour. That's faster than a speeding car.

Insect Numbers

There are over 1 million different types of insects and millions more we haven't discovered yet.

Locusts are a type of grasshopper that eat plants. Billions of locusts can gather together in huge swarms. In just 1 day, they can eat enough crops to feed a large town.

Army ants don't have a home. Tens of thousands of them march around eating every poor insect they come across.

LEFT! RIGHT! LEFT! COME ON, GUYS! IT'S NOT THAT TRICKY TO MARCH WITH 6 LEGS.

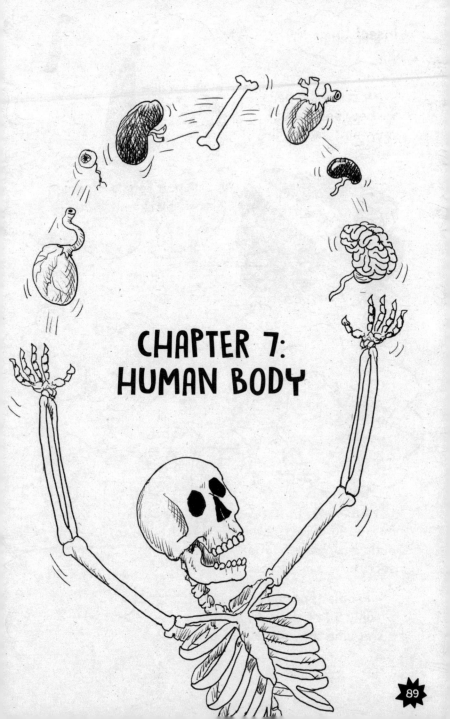

CHAPTER 7:
HUMAN BODY

Sleeping

Most people have between 4 and 6 dreams each night.

Some people dream in black and white.

People tend to remember only 5% of their dreams by the time they get out of bed.

Eating

Your stomach is about the same length as a 30-centimetre (12-inch) school ruler. It stretches if you eat too much.

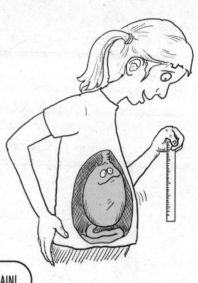

NOT AGAIN!

One man in America had hiccups for 68 years. They began in 1922 and ended in 1990.

After eating, food stays in your stomach for up to 4 hours.

NEARLY TIME TO MOVE ON ...

Burping happens when your stomach needs to get rid of air or gas.

BUURRRRRPP!

Saliva helps you to chew, taste and swallow food. Your mouth produces about 1 to 2 litres (2 to 4 pints) of saliva every day.

HURRY UP, I'M STARVING!

It takes up to 7 seconds for food to travel from your mouth to your stomach.

93

Babies

When newborn babies cry, there are no tears. They start making tears at about 2 weeks old.

A baby's brain doubles in size in the first year of its life.

12 x 12 = 144

When babies are born, they see everything upside down.

THAT'S BETTER!

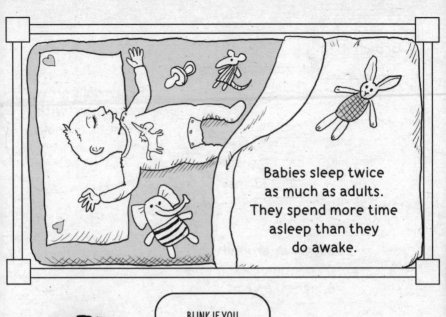

Babies sleep twice as much as adults. They spend more time asleep than they do awake.

BLINK IF YOU WANT SOME MILK ...

Adults blink about 15 times every minute, but babies only blink about twice a minute.

Babies' first 'happy' smiles happen after about 6 weeks, and they start laughing after about 12–16 weeks.

GOO-GOO

GA-GA

People are taller when they wake up. Their backbones spread out when they lie down.

I TOLD YOU I WAS TALL!

Children grow 20 teeth first. When they get their second set of adult teeth, they have 32.

THEY'LL COME BACK SOON ENOUGH.

Your skin is changing all the time. Every month, your old skin wears away and you grow new skin.

NICE SKIN!

THANKS, I GREW IT MYSELF JUST THIS MONTH.

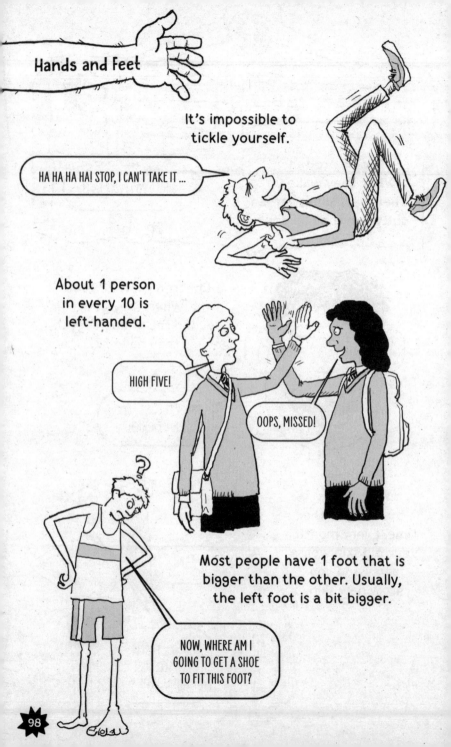

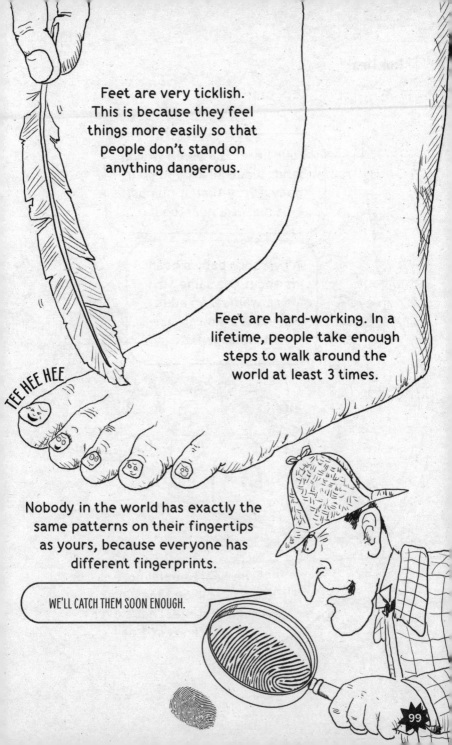

Feet are very ticklish. This is because they feel things more easily so that people don't stand on anything dangerous.

TEE HEE HEE

Feet are hard-working. In a lifetime, people take enough steps to walk around the world at least 3 times.

Nobody in the world has exactly the same patterns on their fingertips as yours, because everyone has different fingerprints.

WE'LL CATCH THEM SOON ENOUGH.

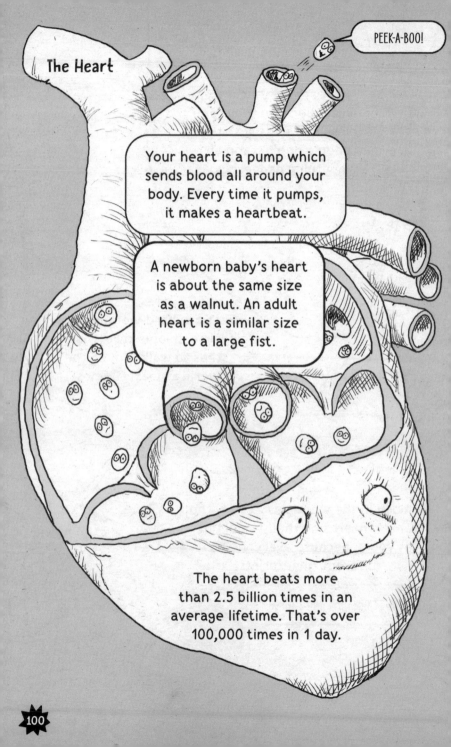

Your heart never, ever has a rest. It will beat for your whole life without ever taking a break.

When you run, it's not just your legs that go faster. Your heart beats faster, as well.

Your heart is powered by electricity, a bit like TVs and light bulbs.

How Long?

Robert Wadlow from America was
2.72 metres (8 feet 11 inches) tall.
That's 1 metre (over 3 feet)
taller than most men.

One woman grew her fingernails
to a combined length of just over
13 metres (42 feet 10 inches),
which is almost as long as
half a basketball court.

One man's beard
grew to over 5 metres
(17 feet 6 inches) long.
That's more than 4
six-year-olds lying
head to toe.

CHAPTER 8:
HISTORY

Wangari Maathai was the first African woman to be awarded the Nobel Peace Prize. She spent her life protecting women's rights and helping people to plant millions of trees in Kenya.

Zenobia was a powerful queen who ruled over a huge area of the Middle East and North Africa nearly 2,000 years ago.

WOOF!

England has had 2 Queen Elizabeths. Elizabeth I was on the throne in the 1500s, and Elizabeth II reigned from 1952 to 2022. Between them, they reigned for well over 100 years.

Having 1 famous author in the family wasn't enough for the 3 Brontë sisters. Charlotte, Emily and Anne Brontë all became very famous. Their books are still read today, over 175 years later.

ANOTHER BESTSELLER FOR THE BRONTË COLLECTION!

Empress Cixi ruled over China for nearly 50 years. She commanded that women should receive an education, not just men.

Amelia Earhart was the first woman to fly on her own across the Atlantic Ocean in 1932.

Odd Jobs

A jester's job was to make people laugh. This medieval comedian could even make fun of the king and queen.

HMPH!

GO AWAY!

In Britain, before alarm clocks, 'knocker-uppers' banged on bedroom windows with a long pole to make sure people weren't late for work.

'Powder monkeys' were young boys who loaded the cannons on big warships with gunpowder.

Vikings

The Vikings were terrifying warriors. They came from the cold, northern countries of Norway, Sweden and Denmark.

The Vikings were famous for attacking villages in their fast longships. Each ship could hold around 60 men.

OI, I'M NOT DEAD. I WAS JUST HAVING A NAP IN MY BOAT!

After their death, some great Viking warriors were buried under a mound of earth with their ship. Others were sent out to sea on board their burning boat.

THAT WAS A CLOSE ONE ...

The Vikings believed in a god of thunder called Thor. He was famous for his powerful hammer.

Some Vikings had really cool names. These include Eric Bloodaxe, Sweyn Forkbeard, Harald Bluetooth and Sigurd Snake-in-the-Eye.

Some Vikings charged into battle dressed in wolfskins to scare their enemies.

When the hot-air balloon was invented over 200 years ago, no one knew whether it was safe. To test it, they sent up a sheep, a duck and a rooster. Luckily, the 3 flying friends returned safely.

WE CAN FLY!

Over 2,000 years ago, the Maya people from Mexico worshipped turkeys.

DON'T WORRY, HE'S COMING BACK ...

The Tower of London's Ravenmaster looks after the birds that live there. Legend says that if the Tower's ravens ever leave, the kingdom of Britain will be destroyed.

Reckless was the name of a US war horse who was made a sergeant for her bravery in 1954. The National Museum of the Marine Corps has a statue of Sergeant Reckless.

BETTER LUCK NEXT TIME.

In 1932, the Australian army declared war on emus because they were eating farmers' crops. After 6 days, the soldiers gave up. The emus had won.

The Celts were an ancient group of warriors. One night they attacked the ancient city of Rome. The guards didn't see them, but the geese did. Their loud honking saved the city.

HONK!

HONK!

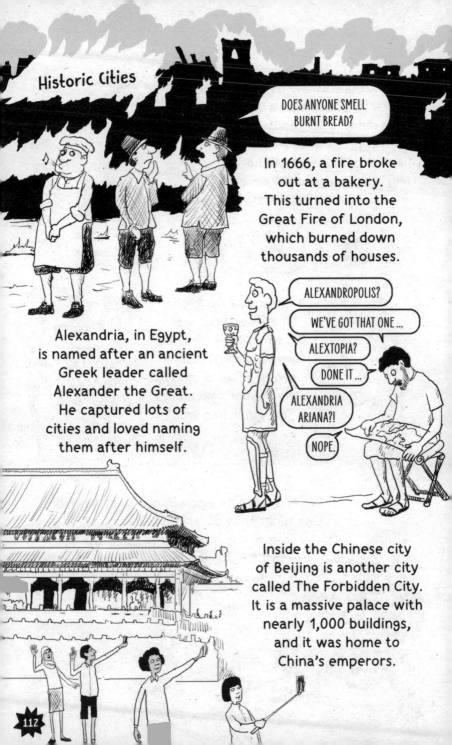

DOES ANYONE SMELL BURNT BREAD?

In 1666, a fire broke out at a bakery. This turned into the Great Fire of London, which burned down thousands of houses.

Alexandria, in Egypt, is named after an ancient Greek leader called Alexander the Great. He captured lots of cities and loved naming them after himself.

ALEXANDROPOLIS?

WE'VE GOT THAT ONE...

ALEXTOPIA?

DONE IT...

ALEXANDRIA ARIANA?!

NOPE.

Inside the Chinese city of Beijing is another city called The Forbidden City. It is a massive palace with nearly 1,000 buildings, and it was home to China's emperors.

Hundreds of years ago, the Inca people built a city in Peru in the shape of a puma. It is called Cuzco and almost half a million people still live there today.

I ♥ NEW AMSTERDAM

I ♥ NEW YORK

When Dutch settlers arrived in North America, they created a city called New Amsterdam. When the British took over, the name was changed to New York.

The people of Venice came up with a good way to stop their city from being invaded. They built it in the sea.

OH, FORGET IT.

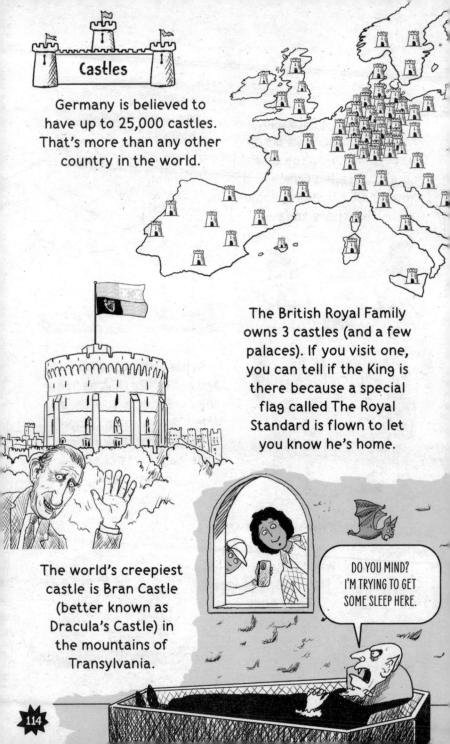

Castles

Germany is believed to have up to 25,000 castles. That's more than any other country in the world.

The British Royal Family owns 3 castles (and a few palaces). If you visit one, you can tell if the King is there because a special flag called The Royal Standard is flown to let you know he's home.

The world's creepiest castle is Bran Castle (better known as Dracula's Castle) in the mountains of Transylvania.

DO YOU MIND? I'M TRYING TO GET SOME SLEEP HERE.

Murder holes were holes in the walls of castles. These let the people inside drop things on attackers' heads.

Castles had drawbridges. These were large wooden doors that were lowered to make a bridge over the water around the castle.

NO NEED TO FLUSH!

HEY, WATCH OUT!

Castle toilets stuck out from the wall. This was so all the waste fell into the moat (the water around a castle) outside.

On the Move

When gold was found in California, 300,000 people quickly travelled there to look for more. That's like a large city moving house!

I SHOULD HAVE KEPT MY MOUTH SHUT...

Criminals usually go to prison. But for 80 years, Great Britain sent more than 160,000 prisoners to live in Australia.

The first modern humans appeared in Africa over 200,000 years ago. From there, they spread out until they covered the whole planet ... except for Antarctica.

WHAT ABOUT ME? IS IT BECAUSE I'M COLD?!

CHAPTER 9:
AMAZING ACHIEVEMENTS

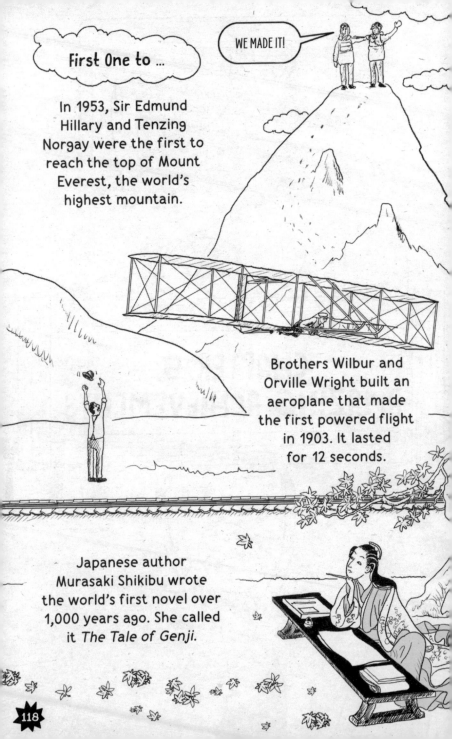

First One to ...

WE MADE IT!

In 1953, Sir Edmund Hillary and Tenzing Norgay were the first to reach the top of Mount Everest, the world's highest mountain.

Brothers Wilbur and Orville Wright built an aeroplane that made the first powered flight in 1903. It lasted for 12 seconds.

Japanese author Murasaki Shikibu wrote the world's first novel over 1,000 years ago. She called it *The Tale of Genji*.

✉ 1
Ray Tomlinson sent the first email in 1971. He sent it to himself, but he can't remember what he typed.

Roald Amundsen was the first person to reach the South Pole. A few years later, he became the first person to fly over the North Pole, too.

In the 18th century, Jeanne Baret became the first woman to sail around the world. She had to dress up as a man because the French navy didn't allow women on ships.

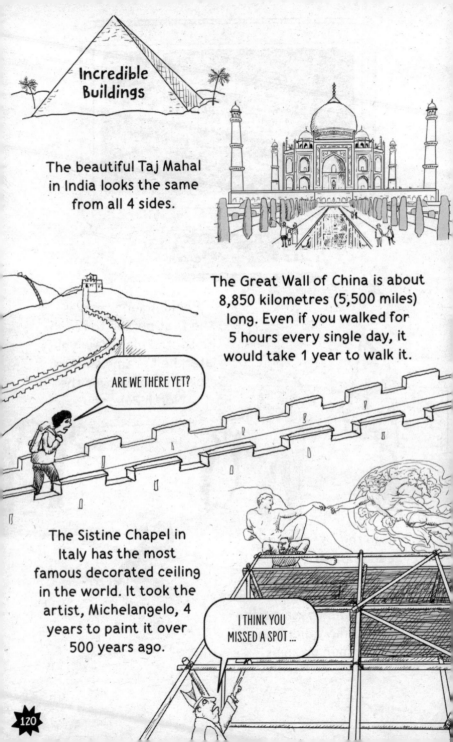

Incredible Buildings

The beautiful Taj Mahal in India looks the same from all 4 sides.

The Great Wall of China is about 8,850 kilometres (5,500 miles) long. Even if you walked for 5 hours every single day, it would take 1 year to walk it.

ARE WE THERE YET?

The Sistine Chapel in Italy has the most famous decorated ceiling in the world. It took the artist, Michelangelo, 4 years to paint it over 500 years ago.

I THINK YOU MISSED A SPOT...

The world's largest pyramid isn't in Egypt. It's in Mexico.

The town of Coober Pedy in Australia is so hot that most people live in underground homes.

Visitors to Sweden can stay in a hotel that's made entirely of ice ... even the beds!

WE'LL SOON GET WARM.

Great Voyages

After his ship was sunk, Poon Lim spent 133 days lost at sea on a wooden raft. He was rescued by some fishermen off the coast of Brazil.

Laura Dekker sailed around the world by herself. She started her epic journey when she was just 14 years old.

The first modern humans managed to voyage to Australia an amazing 50,000 years ago. That's quite some time before people arrived in Europe.

WHAT ARE THEY?

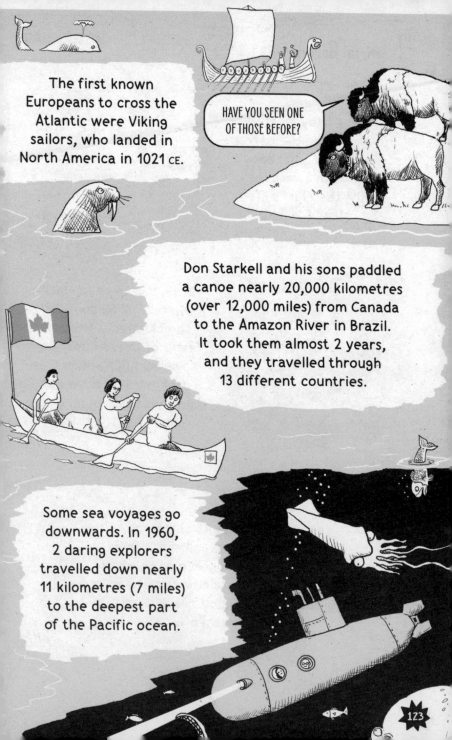

The first known Europeans to cross the Atlantic were Viking sailors, who landed in North America in 1021 CE.

HAVE YOU SEEN ONE OF THOSE BEFORE?

Don Starkell and his sons paddled a canoe nearly 20,000 kilometres (over 12,000 miles) from Canada to the Amazon River in Brazil. It took them almost 2 years, and they travelled through 13 different countries.

Some sea voyages go downwards. In 1960, 2 daring explorers travelled down nearly 11 kilometres (7 miles) to the deepest part of the Pacific ocean.

Animal Heroes

WHO'S A CLEVER BIRD?

When a baby started choking, Willie the parrot screamed, "Mama! Baby!" He won an award for saving the child's life by calling for help.

In 1925, a town in Alaska was cut off by snow and the children were sick. Teams of brave husky dogs covered 1,085 kilometres (674 miles) in snow and icy winds to bring medicine and save the town.

When a great white shark got a bit too close to swimmers in New Zealand in 2004, a group of dolphins appeared and circled round them. The shark couldn't reach them and swam off.

HMPH!

In 1996, a 3-year-old boy fell into a gorilla pen at the zoo. The gorilla picked the boy up and gently carried him to the zoo staff's entry gate.

WOOF! QUICK, OVER THERE!

A man saved a dog from a rescue shelter. Only 2 weeks later, the dog saved the man's life. The clever dog led rescuers to her owner who was trapped in a crashed car.

In 2019, a huge fire was burning around a stable in California. A rescued horse ran back through the flames to save 2 other trapped horses.

Amazing Children

Mozart was a famous music composer. He wrote his first symphony (a large piece of music for an orchestra) when he was about 9 years old.

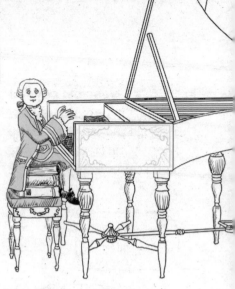

WHEEE!

In 1930, 16-year-old gymnast George Nissen came up with the idea for the trampoline.

I THINK WE'RE GOING TO NEED A SMALLER CROWN ...

Mary Stuart became Queen of Scotland when she was just 6 days old. She is the youngest female ever to become queen.

Jordan Romero climbed Mount Everest, the world's highest mountain, when he was just 13 years old.

In 1983, a 12-year-old girl became the youngest person ever on record to swim across the sea from England to France. It took her 15 hours and 27 minutes. An 11-year-old boy did it in just under 12 hours 5 years later.

ALSO AVAILABLE:

ISBN: 978-1-78055-926-1

ISBN: 978-1-78055-927-8